Acclaim for George Lisi's poetry

George Lisi engages fully with the natural world in these poems, seeing it not through rose-colored glasses, but through the green lens of a poet who speaks the tongue and tone of trees and birds and curling fern, of turning seasons and the winds that wind through it all.

Jane Yolen, author of Owl Moon, Sister Fox's Field Guide to Writing, Things to Say to a Dead Man, *and more than 350 other books*

George Lisi wandered down some seldom traveled pathways during his transformation into a perceptive natural historian and, ultimately, the gentle wizard of his last years, when his poems began to emerge. These utterances are all of the same theme: an abiding joy and respect for the Creation and its deep, often hidden, underpinnings. They encompass falling leaves, ancient rocks, microbes, scarlet tanagers, and the formation of stars. Each is unique, yet all lead toward a deepening awareness of the Everything.

Steven B. Young, Ph. D., founder, The Center for Northern Studies and former Professor of Northern Studies, Middlebury College, Vermont

George Lisi's simple and intelligent language brings with it a balm of healing thought, and an invitation for us to walk the pathways of right relationship to nature, in search of what matters to the heart.

Kristina, Stykos, Chelsea, Vermont

George's words are mossy doorways made of chlorophyll, rain and light. His poems are the birdflight and the nest. Put down a page, dust off the feathers, and return to your life a little greener, wetter, lighter.

JAC Patrissi, author, essayist and fan

George is a gifted craftsman whose tools are the heart and soul of an awakening human being. He shares gloriously the depth with which he feels all of experience and perception in his world, and is able to form language in ways that stretch into the indescribable in our hearts.

Jenny Swing, Maine

George Lisi touches my heart daily with his words. "Through the Gate of Trees: poetry of awakening" has become a vehicle for daily reflection and meditation for me. George Lisi has a connection with nature that is communicated with his poetry and goes straight into my very being. This collection of poems hopefully will reach millions of people. Mr. Lisi is very deserving of recognition for being a master of word.

Eddie Allen Osborn, Oregon

Keep it by my bedside. This is a book of poetry that I read and reread and reread. The words catch me, the way they weave catch me, but what they do to open a world to me is why I read the poems, and then reread them, and then reread them. That deepening love that occurs for me when I read George's poetry brings something special and indescribable to my life, something truly indescribable!

Erika Keller, Vermont

Poetry to soothe your soul. George Lisi has a talent for painting glorious pictures with words and plumbing the depths of one's soul. Anyone who is moved by the beauty of nature will find his poems a restoring balm to a spirit tattered by today's hectic, commercialized world. There are ditties here, as well as psalms, and I find myself returning to his words again and again.

D.R. Cardos, New Hampshire

The Home of Light

Dedicated to the pristine Source of all,
and all of those who seek the real,
within them and without.

THE
HOME OF LIGHT

George Lisi

Earth Heart • East Calais • Vermont

Also by George Lisi

Through the Gate of Trees: poetry of awakening

——————— ——————

text and cover photo copyright ©2014 George Lisi
author photo copyright ©2014 Annie McCleary
design and typesetting by Jane English

published by Earth Heart
PO Box 90, East Calais, Vermont 05650
www.eheart.com

Through the Gate of Trees and *The Home of Light* are available through Wisdom of the Herbs School
www.wisdomoftheherbsschool.com/poetry.html
1005 County Road, East Calais, Vermont 05650

Library of Congress Control Number: 2014959687

ISBN 978-0-934747-36-3
first printing, March 2015
printed in USA by L. Brown & Sons Printing, Barre, Vermont

—— *Contents* ——

Author's Introduction

This book speaks of trees and stars, of this world and the world that floats the world. Of rain, wind and sky. The sun shining through spring leaves. The footsteps of the bee on blossom and winter storm. The first bare tops of autumn trees upon the ridge. The beauty and power of the unseen, inner ecology of the Earth. Of the soul deep joy of colloquy and connection with the inner life of all of these, of the inner journey, the hunger for the real, and the finding of it.

All the tools you need to unfold the true nature of yourself and the world are resident within you. You are the Home of Light. Keep walking until you verify this for yourself.

These poems are love offerings. May you may find them good company as you travel.

—*George Lisi, May 2014*

emerging from the chrysalis
of house and sleep

I step into the dawn
and hear the hidden singers
caroling the darkness
slowly into day

while yet the moon draws
all the gaze of earth

the tender dim
is filled
with many loves

the sweet embracing air
is perfumed with the thoughts
of those
who tend the earth
with heaven in their gaze

and all the lives
that ever lived
are layered
in this moment's deep.

—8/4/13

many the voices
passing

in the
leafy billowing
tap and tingling trees

whispering the sun weaving
shadow caverned
stories
on and on

sighing
of the mystery
of ever dawning bliss

kissing your spirit
softly

through synapses
crafted in a hundred million
murmurings of forest cradled hearts.

— 8/6/13

step softly
under the stars

that sing
to you

even when
they are not seen.

— *10/15/13*

the bird of two worlds
the raven

is flying in the snow

gliding through
the crystal sweep and sway

glinting of
the gold of tamarack
in the dark well of his eye

uttering the air
and holding winter in his bill.

— *10/26/13*

through the passage
and into the wind

a sudden gust
straight out
of the lake's heart

as the liquid curve
of otter

dips
and dives
beneath the wave.

— *10/26/13*

trembling by me in the greenwind
the joe-pye gathers energies
long prepared
to build the daylight ecstasies of bloom

pearly white and tight
the buds
ingathered
forming slow the flowers

I dream with her
in shared joy

the breeze bathing me
in citrus scent of leaves
and thoughts
of rose rays
welcoming the footsteps of the bee.

— 7/16/13

the sweet clover blooms
her fragrant thoughts
into the still dawn air

I pull my chair in close
to her
as to a fire
where we both may warm

we dream among the spires and towers
of her floating city of bloom

her flowers pyrotechnic splendor
bursting softly

in the celebratory sky
of bee space.

—7/17/13

the stillness
at the heart of flowering

is tended by
the ardent
spirits
of the works of life

those artisans of the growth of form
who some call fairy
fey deva
sprite

who labor
in the air of Heaven
with their hands upon the Earth.

— 7/18/13

playing with the
ninety-three million mile light beams

finding my eye
here
then there

through the planet rooted
skyward climbing
trees.

— 7/20/13

gliding on the waters
with my friends

touching a flower like a falling star
breathing in the tang of sphagnum

our spirits bending
in the breeze
that dances with the grassy shore

visiting the green ones
the humble ones
who sing the song
of one world unwounded

under a sky
that opens into endlessness.

— 7/21/13

singing scarlet on the ridge line
the tanager glows
with
a gift
of tropic fire
in the early sun

throat vibrating
song cell deep

and ancient
as a summer day

small
and precious as the air
in the billowing sea of green

under a silent immensity
of pale blue
swept with cloud.

— 7/22/13

powers fly about the world
following the tracks
of dragons in the air

and salamanders gliding
in the molten veins
of Earth

nesting in the curl of clouds
and spreading wide
in every glimmering water

folded close
as moonlight on your skin
to every hurrying heart.

— 7/24/13

three great blue
long legged
fold necked
slow winging herons

following each other
circling in the air

slowly
gaining altitude
and disappearing over the ridge

croaking prehistorically.

— 7/24/13

the majesty moves within these skies
as it has ever done

the door to who you really are
is hidden in plain sight
as it has ever been

recall the welling glory
at the still heart of the dance

and light the fire
that burns 'til all illusion is consumed.

— 7/25/13

let us praise
the viney ones
the creepy crawling tendril clinging
climbers of whatever lifts or leads them toward the sky

and first of these to greet my wakening eyes

the bindweed opening
morning glories
white as moons among the green.

— 7/28/13

as slow the light of Lammas fills the land
the stillness rises through the drowsy trees

a stillness rich with ripening life
and round bellied promise of the fruit

an amber mist of
maturation
fullness
ease

spills like honey
from the throats of bees

and all the patient earth
prepares for rest.

— 8/1/13

there are worlds within worlds
and skies above skies

the incense of the offered lives
goes up
forever

when this becomes
the motion
of your soul

you join the music
serving all
and everywhen.

—8/4/13

roly-polying on the drive
offering white bellied
cat contentment

to the
cloud sailing
openness of sky

rubbing my legs
and kitty bonding
with the press of foreheads
fur to skin

purring mightily
on the surface of the all that is.

— 8/5/13

gravid errantry
of rain returning
water to the earth

straight as spears
ancient as the ever dawning
generative and fertile
both

allow your body
to take heed

the dim of rain
has ever been the home
of gentled hearts

the softly sounding
sacred beats
preceding entry of the light.

— 8/9/13

you dwell upon the doorstep
of the real

the world in fullness
just beyond the outward face

where the ever homing
true winged
heart

recognizes itself
in an astonishment of joy

the fall of rain
has ever been
a soothing hand upon your brow

allow the gentled stillness
to draw you
further
in.

— 8/13/13

touch the world
with thoughts
of love

the lifeblood
of the Earth
flows through veins of consciousness

open the gates
and let the waters
lap the whole world round.

— 8/14/13

honor the spirits
working
in the many realms
that make
a world

the tireless servants
of the Earth

that keep the world
a going.

— 8/14/13

so still
the wuthering of raven wings

traces
their path
through my familiar sky

as I drift
eyes closed
into late summer peace.

— 8/18/13

power moans and hisses
round the fundaments of Earth

the memories of ages
spinning

in the
long embrace
of sun and space

are scribed
within the crystal pathways
of the
planet's skin

the rainbow breath
of dragons
moving
just below the rim of sight.

— 8/19/13

the garden grows
without
within

the twining of the vine

the tree borne
clattering
of the leaves

the thunder
deep
and deepening

the spreading hand
of water
in the low place

and the clambering steep
of stone
that touches sky

all dwell in you
in luminosity

you touch them
with your striding form

and in
the shining field
where light meets light.

— 8/22/13

the moon is drenched
in dawning blue

mist thinned
across the billows

of watery
planet
kissing air

a cape
of trees
appears
swimming into golden.

— 8/24/13

in the dimmy firsting
of the day
a flyer
of the mammal kind

sculpting changes
in the air we share

skin winged by me
closer
than a bird

it wings
a world of echoes
finer tuned than sight

does Alice wonder where you're at?
and shall I fly to be a bat?

— 8/26/13

ride the wave
that
never ebbs

the finned ones ride with you
the winged
the furred the scaled

the small
too many to be seen

the leafy branchers
crystal dreamers

all rising from the deep

to the sound of bells
and blowing conch.

— *8/26/13*

the birds have taught us well

from earliest
turning of the seeds

through caverned floods of green
where every hiddeness
of leaves
was secret
with the glow of eggs

we've watched them
stitching the earth and sky
together

and learned
the freedomed
mysteries of the air

at their
suddenly
skyborne feet.

— 8/29/13

power hums
the spinning
world upholding
lifting of the sacred tide

ocean fathom deep
and current curling
rests
within us

cast as choice
upon the waters
by our every word
and venturing glance.

— 8/29/13

the yellow light
of autumn gales
is glinting in my eyes

the heart of storm
is riding in horizoned clouds

let loose the winds
and blow.

— 8/30/13

fall
into the holy well
of ever now

with the light
that falls to Earth

to sink within
the cricket creaking
blue jay calling

every green horizon's
cells respiring

heart stopping
breath catching

all embracing
multitude of life.

— 8/31/13

under
the sky

of floating clouds
and shallow stars
the round earth

hums.

— 8/31/13

lean into the kingdoms of the wind

the wind
that holds
your body like a cloak

in the long exhale
of the world soul sea

the flowers tremble
in the hand

that ever new
unfolds the light of day.

— 9/2/13

oh best beloved

in all your
conscientiousness

remember
the lift
and glide
the power and sweep

of unbound wings.

— 9/2/13

fellowed in the wind
and
partnered
in the dancing leaves

eye to tree wise
eye
we meet

your warbler world
and mine

are singing
in our common blood.

—9/4/13

the cloudy sheep

trail
their vapory
tails behind them

grazing contentedly

in sweet fields
of autumn sky.

—9/7/13

the days
are flowering
out of timelessness

the ever music
presents
the moment to you

yet again.

— 9/10/13

I looked up
to see her face

framed by leaves
calm as the steady pull
of tides

and close to us
as a million nights of love

speaking peace
and planet tilt towards fall

clear browed messenger
of the great release
and frost
upon the vine.

— 9/16/13

walk the Earth
in time

with the processional
majesty
of the night

the moon pervaded
suzerainty of sky

is but the first
awakening
splash
of the sea that is our home.

— 9/17/13

we're piled like
happy puppies here

bowered together
in the early sun

I sip my tea
with the
wide leaved wavers

the fountaining shrubs
dew drop grasses
the sky ascending viny ones

reflecting the sun
in wet leaf
and curling tendril

lazing in cricket song
and distant busyness
of jays.

— 9/18/13

the early leaves
are sailing
sail away

the winnowing freedoms
of the world
soul wind

sail the ready ones
away.

— 9/21/13

the festival
of equal day and night
is dressed with light

revealing rainbows
living
in the trees

breathe in
the smell of apples
in the leaves

the smell of apples
baked within the house

fall full
into the gravity
of all embracing peace

the harvest home
for the returning dark

that births
the kernelled
sweetness of the Light.

— 9/22/13

listen to their voices

the world wind
and the
leaves

never tire
of their stories.

— 9/25/13

high up
the first bare
antlered tops of trees

process
the ridge
like spirit caribou

dream messengers
of the turnings
of the world
prophesying winter.

— 10/1/13

the fertile dark
of soil
and
patient
watered stone

have somehow thrown
a million flags

of color
towards the sky

waving
from the
twig exultant hands

in the star and sun
beholding
freedoms of the air

carrying the coded
mysteries to our eyes

to charge
our very cells
with tree glad light.

— 10/1/13

how often
have we traveled
with
the mind

amidst the wet and dim
and wind
that does not speak with us

yet always
there

the door that opens
spilling light

that turns the raindrops
into falling suns

as we returning
enter in
and find a fire upon the hearth.

— 10/2/13

the moon has twinned companions
of the trees

their newly bare-branched
shadows

moving
in a fey
transparency of being

through the listening
wakefulness

of moon
declining night.

— 10/11/13

still tarrying
on the surface of this earth

I stretch
my catlike limbs
into eternities on every side.

— 10/13/13

as stars set
in the branchy trees

the land is speaking
only from
remaining leaves

the poplars
glinting gold
in
moonlight

whispering
the stories on and on.

      — 10/15/13

the trees
are gestures
coded in the hills

that dance
the marriage vows

of earth and sky

with every
slow unfolding
twig and branch.

      — 10/15/13

how can such beauty
sing
of love so long

with constant face
above the spinning seas

where first
an ancient cell
awoke to feel her pull

before the land
knew life

and now
we upright
gaze on her

with some return
of her regard

as full
our inner seas
still feel her call

how can such beauty
sing of love
so long.

— 10/16/13

the great uplifted hands
of trees

receive the boundlessness
of sky
for rooted
rolling earth

the leaves remaining
dancers
at that
court of liberation

that we
and all
the circling worlds regard.

— 10/18/13

take heed
of the remaining leaves

their voices
are the
hinge stones of the year

speaking of a journey taken
a task fulfilled
a journey yet to come

of sunlight
starlight
and release

the wind
is dancing
with their freedom

the dappling sun
of their unbinding
plays upon
your face

in ancient beckoning
to a knowing
only found within you.

— 10/21/13

the fierce
exulting wildness of the world

feathered
as the
wings of clouds

is spread across
the sky
in hallowed
elemental joy

the tireless servants
of the world creating wind

still praise
the glory

steady at their tasks.

— 10/22/13

as we descend
this journey with the year

remember
that our eyes

are charged
with color
from the leaves

and we may bathe
within their radiance

through all
the mysteried cloud
of days.

— 10/24/13

hissing like a host
of baby dragons
in the air

the firsting
of the snow

slithers round
the trunks of trees

slips into the curl
of fallen leaves

slides into the elemental ease
of water
and its changes.

— 10/25/13

the plants go traveling
far and away

following their horns of plenty
echoing
in the land
within the land

and so today

lover of water
and dappling light

the mitten leaves
edges scalloped
like a crust

a young witch hazel
waved at me

appearing
in this valley

where none has been
for all these years of noticing eyes.

— 10/27/13

quiet susurrus
of wind and rain

just turned
to giants

casting
crystal gouts
of tintinnabulation.

— 10/28/13

fly your elemental gaze
into
the burning rose
upon the belly of the clouds

float singing roseate

and with your kin

spread
through
the horizoned kingdoms

of departing sun.

— 10/28/13

retrieve your wandering gaze
and listen
deeper

the whetted edge
of the ever new

the keening
all reviving curl

of the endless music
of the
real

closer than your breath
and farther in you.

— 10/30/13

the tamaracks
are dancing
through the thinny time

flickering in and out
bodied and rebodied
in the twilight

their quivering sky antennae
intensely clad
in gold, in gold

visionary as the air
glowing
messengers
of the between

heralding the shaking
of the sky quilt
the piling snow

and dreams
lit by
ice bows and aurora.

— 11/2/13

enfold the
ardent constancy of rain

the home hearth heart
felt in your chest

the reflex
of the steady giving
the ever pouring petalling

of the all
and only mystery
of all enfolding love.

— 11/7/13

Cape Breton
nine years old

high in the green fields
the ocean
huge before me

a goldfinch
bright between
the blue of sky and sea

calling
and dipping
ardent and alone

flying through the vastness.

— 11/8/13

listen deep

expand
your mind's demesne

the spirits
living in the trees

bodiless
untamed

the ardent servants
of the Light
that nurture all that lives

consort with them
as colleagues
and as kin.

— 11/9/13

waking in the dimness
the crystalled
hallowing hush

of the once again
reclothéd trees

the covenant renewed
the spiring
of processing praising firs

lifting resined cones
and snow
remembered needles
skyward.

— 11/10/13

settle in
with
the cinnamon
and ginger moon

the companionable
curl
of the golden
dragon
hissing on your hearth

and prepare a place
for a winter's cricket
and his
song.

— *11/11/13*

follow the trailing fingers
of the wind
across your face

lean close
listen to the voices

of the silver messenger
that has always spoken truth to you

for ages you have wandered
under
the impartial sky

lean closer
listen

and follow the long wind
all the way back

to the primal home
the welling light

cradled deep
within the heart.

— 11/14/13

the dry grass
hissing
sere
between
small waves and sky

rooted
in the waters

the wind of ever
playing
with
the shank bone
shafts

of grass
retreating
home
among the matted roots

the hidden hearth
amidst the tussocks

the rooted toes
touching
cold and cozy mud

that holds the dreams
of frogs and turtles
'til the spring.

— 11/19/13

a kinglet calling
close
within the touching
of the branchy trees

the feathery buzzy ball
of truth

golden
crowned
amidst the gray

the falling
of his voice within our ear

intimate
within the
hush of snow.

— 11/22/13

sup the air
that turns
to fire
in your frame

hear the roaring
of exulting
sky
upon the ridge

turn towards the north
and drink the wind
in neat.

— 11/24/13

the spell is cast
that all
the worlds convene

as snow falls
in the twilight hush

the inner worlds
the crystal worlds

the untold worlds
that float
upon the void like flowers

are all ensorcelled
by the one

and witnessed in your heart
the harmony find
in colloquy
of the intimate unending.

— 11/26/13

hear the praising

the wings and hearts of blessing
leaning
from the windows in the wind

the touch
the kindness
of the world within the world

body forth in you.

— *11/28/13*

the world
blows new born

every moment

from far horizons
deep within the Light

whatever
circumstance
may meet your gaze

I blessed to meet the breath
of corniced stairs
and thrones of ice

the waterfall
descending
from the wild above

patted with hot roses
fresh tracks of mink.

— 12/1/13

sail with
the glinting sable
gliders of the long wing

raven's deft insouciance
of the wild airs

known to you within.

— 12/2/13

the singing endlessness
of being

holds the diuturnity of earth
as a shining bubble
on a stream.

— 12/6/13

the world is moving breath
and breath
and breath about

the receptive hush
of snow

is kindled
with the darkling light
of far off singers

the infrasound
of vastness touching vastness

in the
wide
awakened
traveling of the air.

                    — 12/15/13

liquescent
twig branch root

hanging
like watercolor
from the tree summoning sky

the bark trunk strong ones
soft against
the earth clouds

half transparent in the thaw
melting into peace
and solstice

home and hearth
in shining void
and planet skin.

— *12/21/13*

ever the traveling of the air
inclines the mind
towards inner vastness

the roaring of the trees
beyond the ridges
calming fretful flesh

blessing the heart
with quiet
opening into light.

— 12/30/13

digging for stars and rainbows
in the purlieu
of within

the body drowsy
peaceful
for the nonce

leaning on a bridge between
the senses
and the Light

my eyes
half following
the radiant edge of clouds.

— 12/30/13

weave a gentle mind
around your world

softly as the light
that touches
pale as gold

upon the winged ones
the small ones

the humble great hearts

whose fire burns
a pure and grateful flame

beneath the singing emptiness of sky.

— 12/31/13

winter apples
hanging
red in store

the color
covenant
of the rubicund
and fruitful earth

warming the eye

in spiky branches
starred
with buds

that hold the winter dreams
of emerald leaves
and apple blossoms.

— 1/3/14

processing
with the glaciers
I remember wearing tree

eating rock and sky and water

walking the land
from seed to seed

forgotten in
the red squirrel's cache

my resined cones depending
from my branches

lifted needles rich
with secret
dark green blood

roots rejoicing
in the fragrant earth

passing in and out of form

ever learning
listening
speaking

growing inward
grateful in the vastness.

— 1/5/14

hearts within
hearts
within hearts

so many lifetimes
so many faces
I have seen you wear

helpmates we have been
as friends as lovers
aunts uncles husbands wives

together in
this ancient air again

as we grew
the ever green
unquenchable within

stumbling gliding
trudging flying
towards true north

looking through
each others eyes

we see the stars
again
we taste the endless arc of sky.

— 1/8/14

visiting the waterfall

the massy carapace
of winter's cold

thinned to airy space
and windows

strewn with skeins
of land stuff from the thaw

filled with
watery tumbling tumult

exultant sigil
of eternally
transforming life

inclining mind
to hear
the laughter of the endless music
transfiguring twigs

and bits of leaves
and galaxies
to dust and resurrection.

— *1/13/14*

cleaving finally
through all
the twisted gates of briar

thick as our
rooted dreams of sleep

who is it
who comes to give the kiss?

— 1/16/14

leaning out my window
to breathe
the undivided air

I climb
the eddying trail
of crystal stars
to snow birth clouds

touch winter wood
in every heart of tree

sink ice below
to school with
finny gliders in the dim

enter dreams
of turtles
sleeping in the mud

tune down
to the long rhythms
planet folded in the rock

and company
with all
in company
with sounding light within.

— 1/19/14

listen to the singing

with
the gifted
sifted trees

snow bedizened
swaying slowly

to the music
of the worlds
and worlds and worlds

the skies unending
woven in the bone

of stars and newts
and puppydogs
and stones

calling to you
from the
door above the eyes.

— 1/20/14

the tumbling circumference
of the day

darkening in
the speed and spin
of planet plunge to night

cedes its hilly familiarity

to the polar vertex
of imperious heights of sky

standing under
fast appearing stars
you feel the vertiginous pull

you feel the heat door
open
to the suzerainty of space.

—1/20/14

today my fondness goes
to those
most steadfast of companions

the hosts of the compassion
layered endless
in the Light

the servants
of the ever giving depths
who tend the beauty
of the long
long story.

— 1/21/14

there is a gentle tide
that flows between the worlds

I float upon it

one hand trailing
through the waters
the other curled upon my breast

the sun rises
and the sun sets

the stars wheel
above me
closer than the air

cradled there
I yield
this ardent heart

for my beloved
is so deep a sea
I care not if I sink or swim.

— 1/23/14

lying in the sun
eyes closed well bundled

between the feeder
and the apple tree

the constant sound
of wings
above me

is sign and sigil
of my journey.

— 1/24/14

I remember snow
and snow
and snow again

through all the ages of the world
the cloud light
crystal swirling of the ancient story

held in the hollow
hallowed in the dim

between the earth
and sky.

— 1/27/14

I rest within
the wide company

the endless
undivided fellowship of the real.

— 1/28/14

we sail the waters
of the real

in fellowship
with wings
and wind
and hurrying cloud

we live and breathe
within the waters

the endless beauty
of the deep
that in the end
enchants all hearts.

— 1/28/14

gazing upward at the sky

I lie down with my lover
the familiar blue

we hold our children
in our open arms

smiling as they grow and curl

and sail their freedoms
under sun.

— 1/28/14

we spoke again of incarnation
mentioning its strange
intransigence

yet somehow
in between the words

you justified it perfectly.

— 1/29/14

the morning
is an intimate expanse

the valley whispering
confidences
gentled

in the wing busy
softness of the air.

— 2/2/14

the neighbors
are such
loud-winged noisemakers

the raven
wuffing through the sky

like cerberus bow-wowing
at the hades weary souls

and the wild turkeys
pummeling
the air
from ground to branch

sound like jack
has loosed another giant

clattering
through the clouds
falling earthward with his bean stalk.

— 2/2/14

77

and then one day you realized
the kindness in my eyes
was beside you like a smile

undemanding
whenever you might turn to it.

—2/3/14

sitting in the gloaming
welcoming the evening in

the soft embracing light
is drenched with spring.

—2/3/14

the sky transformed
the ocean into cloud

that rode the winds
to fall as hosts
as endless
ramifying waves of snow

a crystal apotheosis
midwifed by those
beloved servants of the all

who tend
the airs and waters

this ancient dance
is ecstasy for them

rejoice with them
as well
you may know how

in the quiet world
beyond the customary thoughts

the elemental world makes holiday.

— 2/6/14

my sunrise eyes
hold winter pure

and fleeting
gifts
of color

lighting snow new fallen
ruby faceted
in every
tree borne crystal star

the angled branches
dancing
with the beat of wings

in ever new
and ancient dawn

the beauty flying
through the heart
like light

to find a home
beyond the age of earth.

— 2/7/14

the clouds remembered
in the place
we both arise

that I had done my work
my service offered
to the
singing endlessness

and now I was
quite free
to linger here
and sail with them.

— 2/7/14

under the triune
moon orion jove

the quiet multitudes
serve within
the many lights

their raptured stillness
tuning to the singing

of the
ever welling
source of bliss

to fashion matter
out of light

and build
the worlds
that we call nature.

—2/9/14

arising with
the first
pale
wraiths of day
that steal away the lesser stars

I turned
to see bright Venus
burning through an edge of cloud.

— 2/10/14

the slow
music
of icicles

drawn forth by sun
from snow
on snow

sings the sunset light
in crystal
clear newborn.

— 2/10/14

twain and twinned
at uttermost
height
of sky

the moon and jupiter
draw us up
with fierce velocity

escaping
from
the gravity well of earth

to fly into
the dance of spheres
we start to know again.

— *2/11/14*

we say
the clouds
are floating rose
sky traversing amethyst

in truth
unlettered
and unnamed

circling the world
in effortless hegemony

of planet rolling
evening light

our cells
are steeped in it
our spirits recognize

the all pervading
intimacy
of the real

this moment
astonished once again

we open eyes anew.

—2/11/14

outside in the twelve below
I hear the speaking
of the hosts
of sentient wood

the woodpecker's
drumming
resonant upon the branch
tattooing surety of spring

as ever thrumming
round my head
between the apple tree
and seed

the small ones
sun
illumined
surety of wings.

— 2/12/14

and so I walked
the sacred
countenance of moon

in memory
of yours

where so much
truth has been

that all the
holy tides
of earth and heaven
flow within your face.

— 2/12/14

opening the door
within the
belly of the world

the land was sweet and round
and filled with light

this house was blue
and limitless

the sunlight
quiet as
the rise of bliss

kneading
every cell
and thought
and growing thing

to knowing
power and peace.

— 2/15/14

when Earth sinks
from my gaze

I will not disappear

think of me
when the
strong spring sun
shines upon your face

this world is carried
in a shaft of Light

and I will be
what I have always been.

— 2/17/14

follow the skirling
of the
sallow horns

to see the door
stand open in the mind

the gold and silver light
appearing
where the path was dark.

— 2/18/14

I leave you
with the all
and only blessing

the tenderness
infused in the
descending light of Earth

that offers
freedom
undemanding

the ever giving
grace
that floats
the many worlds

that gazes on
the myriad creations

that holds us
in the light

awaiting
our awakening.

— 2/19/14

I remember a night
sixteen
new hampshire

the reconnection
with the beloved
quickening

a thunderstorm
the glory
of the white
out of the dark

the thunder echoing
in ground and grass
and my assembled cells
the same

as rain soaked skin

breathing through
the rain
into the heart of power

the beauty
of the pristine
deathless all pervading.

—2/23/14

in the places
of the Earth
I've walked

carrying the Song
that poured
through hands

opened by the deep
of deeps
remembrance

lifting arms and branch
with all around

to welcome in
the living waters.

— 2/24/14

always up for
fun with spheres

the beloved thought
sublunary
a cool idea

and here we are
the world
beneath our circling moon

while glowing
in the wrack of cloud
and tangling trees and snow

our subplanetary
sun
meets spinning
planet hide of hill.

—2/25/14

spinning
out of mystery

the snows
are elemental
galleons of grace

midwived into form
by clouds

cleansing air
and mind
of fret and heat

opening the way
to the refulgent stillness.

—3/2/14

incarnate
richly layered
beauty in your life

the golden flower
rooted in the formless
opening in the world of form.

—3/4/14

shaking hands
with yellow birches
on the forest edge

feeling the sway
from bough to arm

their branches
sweeping down and up

twigs upturning
fingering
tingling
towards the light.

— 3/6/14

I remember
kissing you by starlight

when all the sweet soul
of the Earth

came rushing
through your mouth

and all the quiet
shining sky
slowly turned in our embrace.

— 3/8/14

the waxing crescent
holding water still

opening hands
and horns

to welcome
all who thirst.

— 3/8/14

this is the season
when the buds
begin to speak

whispering of
the slow unfolding
ardor of the leaves

the ancient energetic
shout of green
that dances with the sun

in evergreen infernos
of primal transformation

opening their quiet hands
and gifting us
a living world.

— 3/8/14

overtired
like a fretful child

the body fading
finding
my way back
to rest and peace
and letting go

pillowed on
the one world neverending

cradled by
the sun and moon
and softly sailing cloud.

—3/8/14

the queen
will have her way

the gardeners
painting
the white roses red

and messengers riding
in furious haste

changing
the numbers
on all the kingdom's clocks.

—3/9/14

pillowed on the air

floating on
the streaming voices
of the kindreds of the Earth

that I have served
in love
as best I may.

—3/9/14

the night unfolds
into a day

of cloud and dim
and silent
sifting snow

the trees
are crystal limned in grace

the dark lit air
receives the speech

of birds
and wings
into the quiet

and on the inner rim
of sight
the patient fire
ever beckoning.

—3/10/14

a long line
a long wind blowing

to this harmony
of purring cat
upon my lap

into matter
from the Light

coalescing dust
and supernova
into Earth

into cell and life
in primal sea

onto land
and flowering
of the million forms

unto this moment
kindred and divergent
we trade our dreams together

cradled in
the dust of stars.

—3/10/14

walking in
the worlds of form

companioned
by the never setting star

that scintillating
goes before my feet

the doorway
to the realms of light

the opening
of the ancient sack

from which
the lake of stars
and all the worlds were spilled.

— 3/11/14

a brash of jays
flaunts by

secure in their many eyes
alert for danger

sky patterned
heraldic

calling through
the subtly softened air

flying through
the gently falling crystal

the warm snow
half melted
at the start of storm.

First in a series written throughout the 3/12 storm.

— 3/12/14

settling to the steady pulse
of storm

the snow
has cloaked
the valley's head in gray

the birds
speak softly
muted in the dim

and all the land
receives
the ceaselessness

the open handed fall
from continent curling
overarching firmaments of cloud.

Second in the storm series.

—3/12/14

the wind arriving
hurling
dragon swirling
hissing streams of snow

swaying waving
greeting
in the sentient trees

as all the crystal celebrants
of air

are
dancing
swooping streaming
in a silvered ecstasy of flight.

Third in the storm series.

—3/12/14

a roaring darkness
deep sung
gloria
of trees beyond the ridge

the hissing touch
of snow
upon my house

of elemental streams
of hidden light

binding out and inward into one.

Last in the storm series.

— 3/12/14

the softly piercing voice
of spring
called to me
from out the snow

the clear 'fee-bee'
cradled in
the elemental power

peeling back my chest
opening my heart
in wordless praise
receptive to the loved one's touch.

— 3/13/14

let the weary body speak
of laying down
of burdens

passed to others
willing hands

of undefended love
surrender and release

of sinking through the Earth
to greet the welcoming glories
of my native place.

— 3/16/14

the trees are waving at you
the birds
fly towards you
carrying the message in their bills

allow yourself
a deeper breath

expand within the true
and freeing air
that breathes
the universe to life

somewhere you know
the dances danced
the lessons learned

are all in aid
of liberation

your nature is of bliss unfettered
as that of all
you dance with here

when you leave the body
you'll remember

let yourself remember now.

—3/17/14

a simple motion
of the heart

an opening upward
of the hands

a standing
firm upon the earth

to feel the many lives around

to gather them smiling in
and breathe
your greeting smiling out.

—3/18/14

the wind arriving
with the
meeting of the airs

blowing clean as stars
straight from
the beginning of the world

folding us inward
to the
stillness
wrapping us in presence

the elementals
whispering to us
in the silvered voice of air.

—3/19/14

the many faces
of your
sky reflective sea

are cradled
by the peaceful deeps

the slow and steady strength
of currents
traversing many worlds

the sounding
of the great ones
in profundus.

— 3/20/14

folded in
a plenitude of sky

I join my gaze
with the compassionate hosts

the never sleeping
guardian eyes of love
that bless
the Earth unceasingly

as I both sip
and offer out
the ceaseless manna
pouring from the inner skies.

— 3/20/14

those white pines
held me first

young and lying soft
among their resined duff

listening to
the soughing of the wind
from everywhere to always.

— 3/21/14

lying with you
on the earth
that pressed us back

our heads so full of green
with every breath

we sank into the ground
and sailed
the blossoming air

when rumored
through the drum of hills
we heard the beat

the coming
of the land incarnate

rushing by us
shaggy with the moor

and dark out of their eyes
a wild imperious
glance of praise.

— 3/21/14

two-legged talk
is all of snow on snow

yet lifting
in the growing days

returning crows
are speaking to me

first to breast the hills
since autumn's haze.

— 3/22/14

turning with you
smiles half hid
amidst the stars

hushed beneath
the holy blaze

feeling your
heart beat
close beside me.

— 3/24/14

feet pressing
on the Earth
that presses back

I walk as well
the timeless worlds
that hold the worlds of time

the listening lives
all round
of branch and fur and wing

are travelers
on a road
that blossoms upward

beholding them
in time and out
I chorus with them

singing to them
in a chord of many worlds
the glory of their sacred lives.

—3/24/14

today a day
for golden
inwardness of bloom

cut the knot
step through the door

you have it in you
to consent
to that
which patiently abides

in each pion
quark charmed particle

heart
spring is ever flowering

somehow wildly hear the call
remembering.

—3/26/14

something in the ease
of the first
full bubbling song

feathers
new upon
the moving throat

purple finch
untying knots
in winter winded ears

snow still below
endless blue above.

—3/27/14

that high valley
chalice of the sky
mountain circled

witnessing the many footsteps

unlettered
speaking only streams
and peaks and trees

heard and hearing
holding you then

in colloquy of souls
perhaps unknown to you

now witness
of the inward birth

biding with you
for the journey

crystal arms
outspread
reflecting light to light.

—3/27/14

sometimes I gaze
in wild surmise

the small gifts
from a friend

I saw the beauty
I saw the atoms

differently ranged
in paper
pressed flower

pressed marks of words
the sealing plastic

I taped them
here and there

small art
from a dear hand

it took me months
to realize
these are bookmarks.

—3/29/14

in every moment
dulcet from
the ever open gates

the trumpets
hold sustained
the many worlds

ever witnessing
offering
the many
shifting colors

offering
the hidden gift
of life itself uncovered

to all who finally will.

—3/30/14

slow flowing mystery
of sap
and dreaming bloom

kept safe for now
within the house

is outside waiting
like a wave

that rises root to leaf
to spreading seas of green.

—4/1/14

a robin fat
and red
and belly full
of promised spring.

— 4/2/14

listening to
the new wings

the wings like voices
anciently declaring
in each
species flight

honed
to just this
in the long dance of the years

evolving with the earth and sky
cleaving the air
in subtle beats of time

individual as call or song.

— 4/3/14

owning the soggy ground
with your coruscating ebony

grackle long tailed sleek
returning
iridescent color
from snowlight dim

herald of self assurance

you turn
the early chill
into a strutting fair of life

before you fly off
with your gang of four

you tilt your head my way
meeting me
within your pale gold eye.

— 4/9/14

the chalice of this moment
offered up

with wind and wheeling bird
with water
falling voice

and all the lives
that ever lived.

— 4/15/14

this day reveals
the intimacies of earth

the places where the snow
is last to melt

where spring yet stretches
soft and folded
in her sleep.

— 4/15/14

spinning round
upon my spindled core

I roll the moon
behind beloved trees.

— 4/17/14

feel the swing and sway
of longer days

arching through
the aching heights of sky

to ground in earth
like rainbow

glimmering through
the still bare trees.

— 4/18/14

the green will come
but now

release yourself
into
the glory

of the rain dark
cloud speaking
light
upon the land.

— 4/19/14

I rest within
the faithfulness of wood

the endless
standing crowd upon the earth

that through the winter storms

carries safe
the emerald flower of the world.

— 4/20/14

it is a day
made out of light

as I roll
tree shaggy

and shadow hilled
towards distant night

the moon
is swimming
in a sea of blue.

— 4/20/14

the land well rested
from the snows

stretching herself
in waterfalling sigh

and soft
of crystal airs
amidst bud fingered trees

her leaf strewn flanks
pungent with
the sleek of hills

unfolding
green spelled

root upreaching
sorceries
timeless in the Light.

— 4/22/14

the world
I see

is brewing
up another batch

of slightly modified eternity.

— 4/24/14

speeding with
the light
of more than suns

the ever giving
streaming
through the earth

eternity and home
inviting

embracing all
with open arms.

— 4/24/14

the last
gray raft of ice
dissolved last night

this morning
in the early light

silver wakes
appearing

speeding
back and forth
within the narrows

pushing
water fast
just for the hell of it

liquid liberated
otters
making waves.

— 4/30/14

a robin singing
from
the ever fall of rain

and trees
that grow
and conjure to the sky

as if the hidden peace
within the heart
gave voice.

— 5/1/14

this Earth
is not one thing

the high uplifted
deeply plunging
mass of planetary stone

of rainbows
also is she wove

of solitary flowers
blooming that
no eye has ever seen

glory in the Earth
as now she is

that you may
recognize her face
as swift she changes.

— 5/2/14

the eye of water
opened
in the land

my lovely friend
of otter rolls
and beaver paths

reflecting all
and holding
all the messages

of all the
holy earths and seeps

and waterfalling
tree held lands around.

— 5/2/14

heart aura underwings
rose as its breast

the new arrived grosbeak
flutters to feed

gentle to prise
the generous seed

within a gesture
of my hand.

— 5/3/14

I remember
all the blue yonders

the calling of the wild song
in heaven
earth

and all
the far fair regions
of the one true real

and of the wildest call of all
issuing always
from the center

from the pristine glance
beckoning us always
further in.

—5/5/14

I feel the lifting
of the tide beneath my keel

remembering journeys
on the wide
and starry seas

the Earth itself
a glint of foam
in starlight.

—5/7/14

pair flying
ravens dance

and whisper
feathers through the air

shining sunward
wheeling diving
curving

following each other
closer
than a wing

the strong and wise ones
feathering
their delight

in free and air
and two.

—5/11/14

soon I go to rest
the rest

which is the sweet seed
of adventure

journeying
with the companion

through vastnesses
of Light
and whispering glades of stars.

— 5/15/14

at the heart of the world
there is a rose

the ageless
open secret
that you carry
with you everywhere

climb the tower
to the door above the eyes

and follow the thinning
of the thousand petals
to the dawn.

— 12/2/13

we come
from where the myriad creations
resolve into the singing light

and all the life around us here
from tree to bedded crystal seam

remembers deep the echo
and dreams upon
that music still

the tale
of all the worlds
within that aspiration writ

all the lives here
follow us
and hold us up
the kinned foundation of our deepest walk

to travel
with liberated inner gaze
the road towards that return

and hold
the growing light of heaven
in our gaze upon this earth.

— 12/12/13

Index of First Lines

The Home of Light
Afterword
by Annie McCleary

The poems of *The Home of Light* were written between July 2013 and May 2014. During that last year of his life, George Lisi was increasingly ill, and he wrote these poems with a purpose that belied his increasingly weakening physical state. George left his body on July 3, 2014, at the height of a wind and rain storm. A naturalist, poet, meditator, and teacher, George was a gentle soul of profound perception, dearly loved by his community.

George carried a high spiritual awareness that permeated his teaching, his poetry and his daily life. A confidence in each person's ability to unfold their own true nature was at the back of all George's interactions and many will recall his quiet encouragement and support. He related directly with the inner life of all beings and of the Earth itself, rejoicing in the constant colloquy of soul to soul. The kernel of his life was working deeply within the Light in service to all beloved beings in these rapidly changing times.

George enjoyed a lifelong love of words and his writing arose from a lifelong love affair with the Earth. His poetry celebrates beauty, depth and immediacy of connection with all of life, keen observation, inner integration, and spiritual awakening.

George and I co-taught at Wisdom of the Herbs School where George led Nature Adventure walks into the deep woods, up streams, and into beaver meadows and fen. He was highly respected and well-loved by our students who he delighted with his encyclopedic scientific knowledge, his passion and gentle humor, and his expansive view of inner and outer realities.

Annie McCleary and George Lisi enjoyed a 21 year long rich relationship as friends, colleagues, neighbors and confidants. They walked together practically daily, exploring the richness of the natural world, covering a couple of thousand miles over the years, usually within a ¼ mile of their homes. Annie is Director of Wisdom of the Herbs School in Woodbury, Vermont.

George Lisi taught with Annie McCleary at the

Wisdom of the Herbs School

nature ~ healing ~ sustainable living
www.wisdomoftheherbsschool.com

Wisdom of the Herbs School offers unique experiential programs embracing the wild herbaceous plants, shrubs and the trees, holistic health, and sustainable living skills, valuable tools for living on the Earth in these changing times. Participants learn through herb walks and nature adventures, communion with Nature, lecture and discussion, hands-on wild harvesting and preparation of wild edibles and herbal home remedies, with intention and gratitude.

Our School encompasses much more than herbs - we offer perspectives on healthy life-style practices, primitive and homesteading skills, and the timelessness of communion between Nature and self. The emphasis is on integration of the intuitive and scientific, all in a relaxed, magical and grounded atmosphere.

Wisdom of the Herbs School is located in Woodbury, Vermont, on the east side of the Green Mountains, 20 minutes north of Montpelier, and just over an hour from Burlington. The surrounding exquisite wild lands offer a series of beaver ponds, dramatic falls and streams, a richness of open and wooded territory, and welcoming nature beings.

Our small class size maximizes the transformation that comes from multidimensional adventuring with the plant people.

Through the Gate of Trees and *The Home of Light* are available through Wisdom of the Herbs School — www.wisdomoftheherbsschool.com/poetry.html

Donations in memory of George Lisi may be sent to:

Wisdom of the Herbs School, 1005 County Road, East Calais, Vermont 05650